Young Ted

Irish Traveler

Young Ted

Irish Traveler

MY WAY

A story of faith, love, and friendship

XULON ELITE

Xulon Press Elite
2301 Lucien Way #415
Maitland, FL 32751
407.339.4217
www.xulonpress.com

Paperback ISBN-13: 978-1-6628-5064-6
Ebook ISBN-13: 978-1-6628-5065-3

Table of Contents

Introduction

Ted Daley was an Irish Traveler his entire life. He lives and breathes this life. This has been a way of life for many, not only here in the United States, but in the world. Many cultures and lifestyles that have been forgotten in the pages of history. Ted would like to accomplish many things by writing this book.

First, Ted wants to preserve the cultural heritage of Irish Travelers here in the United States. As many cultures have been lost and forgotten in our rapidly changing world, the Irish Traveler made its mark in this time of history. Many people are not even aware that the cultural heritage of the Iris Traveler existed.

Secondly, Ted wishes to set the record straight. For a number of people that think they know about Irish Travelers, they have a negative view of the traveler. Of course, like any culture, there are some bad apples that have done things to give them a bad reputation. However, the majority have lived good productive lives and positively contributed to society.

Thirdly, the reader has an opportunity to see 20th century American life through some of the experiences of Ted Dailey Jr. Ted is a colorful individual. When reading this book, one can take a few moments to enjoy the life and legacy that he has lived life in the fullest sense of the word. Life gives all of us opportunities to face difficult circumstances regardless of what time and place we live. Ted took on many challenges during this time in history. It also gives the reader a chance to reflect upon the many changes that have taken place in our present society.

Fourthly, the book gives us a relevant message for today. In the midst of so much conflict and division, we can hold true to our identity and be proud of who we are, yet be respectful and enjoy the presence of others outside our identity group. Most Irish Travelers were Catholic. There were other Travelers, English, Scottish, and Romany, who were basically protestant. As many know in Northern Ireland, war raged between the Irish Catholics and Protestants for years. Ted, despite his strong identity as an Irish Traveler, related well and respected other faiths. Ted has a strong faith as a Catholic, yet wants people of all religions to get along and live in peace. He lived that philosophy as an Irish Traveler.

Chapter 1
Family History

Ted's Parents were Angeline and Ted Daley. Angeline was born Angeline (Angie) Finney on August 3rd 1907 in Coventry England. Her family moved from Ireland to England. She was an English Traveler and then moved back to Ireland. Her family sold horses and the market for selling horses was better in Ireland so they came back to Ireland. Ted's dad Ted was born on August 22, 1907 in Rohdes Ireland (Offley county). His dad was born Edward Mark Daley, but known as Ted. In Ireland many people named Edward have their name shortened to either Ned or Ted. Ted was an Irish traveler. Ted and Angie did not know each other in Ireland. They both came to the United States in 1914 at the age of 7. As most immigrants, they came through Ellis Island in New York. A relative set them up to meet. After a short time, they were scheduled to get married. Ted, however got scared and did not want to get married because his twin brother got married and was divorced shortly after the wedding. He did not want to end up like his brother. They did end up getting married on June 15, 1928 by the Justice of the Peace. Later, they had their marriage blessed in a Catholic Church in Los Angeles, California When they moved there from New York. Angeline Died in June 12, 2008 and Ted senior died November 15, 1988.

Angeline and Ted Daley had three children; Susan, Jane and Ted. Ted was the youngest of the three children. Ted was born on April 3, 1937 in Wichita Kansas. His full name was Edward John Daley Jr. Like his father, they maintained the Irish tradition of using the abbreviated name of Ted. Some who do not know Ted think his full name is Theodore, which it is not. Although his legal name is Edward everyone knows him as Ted. Therefore, we will use the name Ted throughout this book.

Many of the travelers lived in trailer parks, as did his parents. The manager of the trailer park was Mr. Kennedy. He was friends of the Daley's. He became the god-father to Ted. Ted always had an affinity to the name Edward John Kennedy. He loved the Kennedy family also because they were Irish Catholics.

Ted knew his bride most of his life. Many Irish travelers would often get together, therefore they knew other Irish families very well, including Sue's family. In the summer of 1956 Ted and his family went to South Dakota with other travelers. At that time is South Dakota Ted saw Sue McDonald and got reacquainted with her. She too was from Fort Worth Texas. Ted said to Sue, "I like you, do you like me? Well, let's get engaged!" Although, Ted knew other women, he was engaged to Susan McDonald. 5 days before the wedding Ted called it off. He was 19 years old and wanted to get out of it because he was scared. Ted's dad had a heart to heart talk with Ted. He said, "you can't treat a travelling girl like that"! Both Ted's dad and mom along with Ted, went to the home of Susan McDonald, and spoke with her parents. The wedding did take place on the scheduled date. The wedding took place on November 26, 1956 at St. Helen's Catholic Church in Shively, Kentucky. Many Irish, Scottish and English travelers came to the wedding. That must have been the right decision, because they have been married over 66 years. Of this union there were 4 children, 21 grand-children and 62 great grand-children and 1 great-great grand-child. The grand-children were born in 6 different states. In 1984 two grand-children were born New York city and baptized at St. Patrick's Cathedral in New York.

Ted and Sue lived in many places throughout the United States. As travelers, they would go north in the summertime and South for the winter. They would work at different jobs in their travels. Six months after Ted got married to Sue they lived in a trailer park in Edinburgh, Indiana. His parents and uncle also lived in separate trailers in the same park. The owner of the park had a 3 year old horse in the pasture that was never ridden. One day the owner of the park mentioned to Ted's dad about that wild horse and how he wanted someone to break it to be a riding horse. Ted's dad said, "Don't worry, my son will do that for you". New you have to understand Ted never touched a horse in his life. Because of Ted's devotion and respect for his father, Ted agreed to break the horse. One day Ted and his father went with the owner of the horse to the pasture where the horse was eating. They rounded up the horse and Ted's dad bit the horse's ear and it settled down. Then Ted got on the horse and the horse bucked him off. He went flying 10 feet in the air and hit the ground. It felt like concrete it was so hard. They rounded up the horse again and Ted's dad said, "Son, you can do this". Ted's dad bit the horse's ear again, settled it down and Ted fearfully got back on the horse. Despite all the bumps and bruises, Ted broke the horse to be a gentle riding horse. Even his wife Sue rode the horse without getting bucked off. In return the owner gave Ted $150.00 off of rent. In those days rent was 50.00 a month. That was very expensive. Ted in turn gave the one month rent free to his dad and uncle besides one month for himself.

Another place they lived was Havana, Illinois. On November 10, 1960, while living in Havana, Ted and Sue wanted to watch the television show Wagon Train. In those days there was UHF and VHF T.V. signals. Wagon Train was on VHF but they only had UHF. Ted wanted to put up an additional T.V. antenna so he could get more channels and the show Wagon Train. Ted crawled on the roof to put up the antenna 30 feet up in the air. What he did not realize was an electric cable that hung lower than the 30 feet. When the metal antenna hit the electric cable 4,440 volts of electricity went through his body. His wife Sue grabbed him when the electricity hit him. The electricity then hit Sue and blew out her forehead. To this day she has a scar on her forehead from the jolt of electricity. Ted's heart stopped beating and he just vibrated on the ground. Sue ran down to the 3rd trailer house where there was a high line man there by the name of Ed White. Sue said, "My husband just got electrocuted". Ed White came running, and arrived within three minutes. It was as fast as lightening. If he was any later, Ted would have been dead. Ted's two year old son came running to Ted and said, "Wake up daddy, wake up!". Ed turned Ted over and hit his back. Ted came to a little bit and said don't stop. Ted was in a deep darkness and had blood all over him. He pumped air in his lungs and then was brought to the hospital along with his wife Sue. At that time Ted and Sue had two children. Ted prayed "Dear God, please don't let me die. Let me see my children be raised". The neighbors took care of their children while they were in the hospital. Needless to say, they never watched Wagon Train that night. For the next 1 ½ months when Ted would go to work, he thought how lucky he was to be alive. He noticed the grass and corn of the fields, the clouds in the sky and other ordinary things in his surroundings. He appreciated the little things around him.

Ted always had a special affinity to President John F. Kennedy because he was an Irish Catholic. When Kennedy became president, Ted wanted to become a good citizen of the United States of America. He applied for a Social Security number and card. He paid taxes and followed the laws of the land. Ted was living in Kansas City at the time. The day President Kennedy got shot has been burned on his brain.

It was a rainy and dreary day in Kansas City and some of the travelers got together for a few drinks. Many protestant travelers liked to hang around the Irish travelers because they liked to have a few beers. Johnny Goorman and cousins Pete Daley and George Holiday met Ted at a local pub in downtown Kansas City. Johnny Gorman was a Catholic but George was a protestant Scottish traveler. George did not drink a lot, but when he did, watch out. As this group of guys left the pub and when they just turned a corner, someone yelled out that President Kennedy was shot. Those words were like a knife that ripped through Ted's heart. They kept walking in shock to their trucks. Johnny Gorman got in his truck screaming and wailing as he hit the dashboard of his truck. He kept hollering: "The protestants killed him". George, the protestant, was half drunk and said, "I didn't want him to die". It was a very sad day. Ted took George home. Ted knew that in a world of violence and sadness, there must be something more to this world. Where was God in all of this mess?

Chapter 2

The Holy Spirit is Moving

Travelers always moved around to different parts of the country depending on work and the climate. Travelers, many times, lived in trailer parks. His parents were no different. During WW II his parents lived in a big trailer park in Savannah Georgia. There were tents on the side of the trailer. His father worked in the shipyards in Savannah Georgia. In 1942-1943 Ted attended Sacred Heart Catholic School for his education. Ted received the sacraments in the Catholic Church at different locations. Ted was baptized as an infant in Wichita Kansas. Like most Catholics at the time, he was baptized within a week of his birth. He made his First Holy Communion at the age of 7 during a private ceremony at a convent with Catholic Nuns in attendance along with a young Jewish boy. The reason he made his First Holy Communion in a private ceremony at the convent, so he could be confirmed with the regular class at the parish church with the bishop. Ted had to catchup on some studies that the other children already went through. There was some thought that the Jewish boy was baptized as a way to protect him from the Nazi's in Germany. This was during WW II where the fear of Nazis was a real threat to our world. A short time later, Ted was confirmed in the Catholic faith at Sacred Heart Catholic Church. And of course, Ted was married on November 26, 1956 at St. Helen's Catholic Church in Shively Kentucky.

Besides going to a Catholic school, Ted attended mass each Sunday with his family. His faith meant a lot to him throughout his life. The family prayed together and he learned his prayers in the faith as he grew in age. Ted went to prayer meetings and sang at different churches. Although Ted grew up to be a strong Catholic, he also lived among protestants. It was through this living experience that Ted had a deep respect for protestants and those not of the Catholic faith.

Ted's parents thought that Ted would be a priest. At the age of 12 Ted prayed earnestly NOT to become a priest. Ted prayed, "Dear God, please do not let me become a priest. If I become a priest none of my Scottish friends would have anything to do with me". Well, God answered his prayer and he never became a priest.

Although Ted did not become a priest, he was no stranger to religion. Ted attended mass regularly, contributed generously to the parish, read the bible and attended prayer meetings. Ted specifically remembers reading the bible passage from 1 Corinthians 13 about love. Love is patient and kind. In the end three things that last; faith, hope, and love, and the greatest of these is love. Ted reflected on this passage a lot. So many other things were bothering him at this time in his life. He was wondering if he was in a state of depression. He was worried about many things, including: how much money he should give to the church, what if he lost money, did he pay all of his income taxes, are the communists taking over our country, are the communists taking over the church? The list went on and on. He thought his life was coming to an end. Ted continued to read the bible and pray. Ted was living in New Ulm Minnesota at the time. He was in bad shape. He wanted to talk to someone so he went to a local pub. There was an older man there having a beer and Ted thought he was a bishop. He looked very similar to a bishop I knew in Iowa. Ted spoke with him and he gave Ted some counsel. Ted also put $500.00 in the door of the rectory. He went to confession to the priest and the priest suggested to see a tax man to relieve him of this burden.

A short time later Ted went to Cherokee Iowa to see his parents. Ted stayed overnight with his mom and dad. They lived in a trailer park. Bells from the church would ring early and he would go to mass. One day, while visiting his parents, he felt a strong urge drawing him out of the trailer. There was a set of railroad tracks that ran behind the trailer court. Ted walked on those railroad tracks that led him right to the church. The doors were open on the church and he felt God was calling him for some reason. Ted then walked in the church. Ted walked up to the altar. At this time, he was shaking badly. He knelt down in front of the altar and said a prayer. Then he got up to kiss the altar. When he kissed the altar, he looked up and saw the tabernacle. The tabernacle is where the consecrated host is safely preserved. As Catholics we believe it is the body, blood, soul, and divinity of Jesus Christ. Ted then saw a light coming out of the tabernacle. It was 3or4 feet long waving in the air. It was a golden light coming right towards Ted. The light went right inside of him. Ted lost strength, passed out, and fell right on the floor. After sometime went by, which he does not know how long, he looked up in the dome of the church. There he saw a dove. The dove is a symbol of the Holy Spirit. He truly felt the Holy Spirit came to him in a personal and unique way.

As Ted laid on the church floor many random thoughts came in his mind and he hollered out many things. He hollered to his protestant aunts that he loved them. He remembered Bobby Holiday, and said, "Jesus has always loved you uncle Bob". He did not know Bobby meant so much to him. Bobby was 100% protestant, but a good man. When he felt his strength coming back, he started hollering even more. He was hollering for his uncles and aunts; especially for the three that had muscular dystrophy. Other people came to mind that he did not think about in years. To this day he has no reason why he said these things. Ted was so exhausted he felt he put in a whole day of work. He even felt uneasy, like he made the Holy Spirit come to him.

After more strength came back to his body, he slowly sauntered to his parent's house in the trailer park. Ted then spoke to his mother that the Holy Spirit had come to him. He asked his mother to call his wife Sue and tell her where he was at. Ted thought he was dying. His breathing became slower and slower. Ted said, "Jesus take me".

Ted's mom and dad thought he flipped out. They did not know what happened to him. They took Ted to a psychiatric hospital. They saw a priest-chaplain at the hospital and spoke with him. His mom and dad said to the priest, "I think Ted lost his mind. He thinks the Holy Spirit came to him". The priest said, "Do you doubt that the Holy Spirit cannot come to him"? His parents did not know what to say. A few days later he went back home to New Ulm Minnesota. The day the Holy Spirit came to Ted was one of the most important days of his life.

Throughout Ted's life there were a number of times that Ted sang for groups of people. On a number of occasions, Ted was able to lift the spirits of so many people through song. One of the groups that Ted sang for were Catholic nuns from Amarillo Texas. One of the nuns was so impressed with Ted's singing that she wrote a card back to Ted that said, "Your singing is ministry to the soul". Ted never thought of that before, but appreciated the insight she gave him to continue to touch people's lives.

Ted did not become a priest, but Ted truly believes that God has used him to touch the hearts of people of many religions and nationalities. Through music Ted was able to communicate between Catholics and protestants. They are Ted's brothers and sisters in Christ. Catholics receive Jesus at the mass in holy communion. It also says in the bible that not by bread alone does a person live, but by every word that comes forth from the mouth of God. The protestant receives Jesus in the word. Most are baptized by water; some are baptized by desire. Ted's desire is that we have respect for one another so we can live in peace. Through song, Ted touched the hearts of many.

Chapter 3

The Traveling Man

Much of this book speaks about travelers. When I speak about travelers I'm not speaking about a person or group of people going from one destination to another destination. I'm speaking about a culture; a way of life. In some ways it is difficult to define the culture of travelers. There were different groups of travelers. There were Irish travelers, Scottish travelers, English travelers and Romany travelers. The Irish travelers were broken down into smaller groups. The group that Ted belonged to were the Irish Green Horns. The Irish travelers were basically Catholic, the rest of the travelers were predominantly protestant. Regardless of religion or origin, the traveler would travel around in groups, work and live the best they could to support their families. Many did not have permanent homes. They did not put money in the bank but kept it in secret hiding places. A lot of the traveler's lifestyle has changed over the years. This is why Ted wants to preserve this heritage through the writing of this book. Most now have settled down and buy homes for their families. They use banks and pay income taxes. They want to be honest good American citizens. Ted's dad said, "There is no country in the world like the United states of America".

There is a history to their traveling lifestyle. Back in Ireland when the potato famine gripped the entire nation, they had to leave their homes in search of food. Some burned down their homes so the English would not get them. The Irish travelers were in England so long, they became known as English travelers, even though they originated from Ireland. Many traveled to England, never to return to their native home. Many Scottish travelers first came from Ireland and ended up in Scotland. The Romany's were English gypsies that go back almost 2000 years.

Over the years the travelers had a bad reputation. Some people considered them to be thieves, uneducated, and worthless. Some considered them to be the lowest culture in the country. This is where Ted wants to set the record straight. They were good people. To know them is to love them. Ted believed in his heart that you treat a person like you want to be treated. You need to treat people right. Sure, there were some bad apples in the bunch, but over-all they worked hard and contributed positively to society. Any culture has a few bad apples. For the most part 90% of travelers were uneducated. Many, after they learned to read and write never went back to school. Those who did pursue an education did very well for themselves. Some became doctors and lawyers. Some joined the military to serve our country.

Ted's grandfather had a saying about travelers: He is not a rich man, he is not a poor man. He is not a beggar, he is not a thief. But he has a dollar to lend and a dollar to spend; and a dollar to give to the poor. The travelers hung out together; they were like family. In the summer of 1946 Ted was 9 years old. His family stayed in a trailer court in Detroit Michigan. The trailer court held about 20 trailers. Travelers occupied all 20 trailers. Ted's family was the only Irish traveler in the park. All the rest were English and Scottish travelers. They had the best of respect for his dad and the entire Daley family despite any religious or nationality differences. Ted learned to love them as brothers. This book has relevancy for today because it can teach us that we can live together peacefully and still be of different origins. As one can recall, there were race riots in the 60's. Some of the racial tensions exist to this day. Ted even wrote to President Clinton if there was anything the travelers could do to lessen any racial tensions. Ted did not like hatred.

Travelers worked hard and did a variety of jobs as they moved from town to town. Ted's dad painted barns. One of his dad's coworkers was an English traveler, named Fred Turner, who was a war hero. He was a Sargent in the army during WW II. When they started out, they painted the barns by hand. Later they used high pressure orchard spray pumps to paint the barns. They could paint a barn in 1 ½ hours. They painted many barns in Illinois, Indiana, Michigan and Wisconsin. One day they were leaving Savannah Georgia heading north to paint barns. Before they left Savannah, they bought paint at the shipyards at a cheap price. It was only $1.00 per bucket. They bought 50 buckets of paint because it was such a good deal. Uncle John was driving the truck with all the paint. His sister Jane was riding in the truck with Uncle John. Jane was 12 years old. Ted and his mom and dad were driving ahead of the truck. They were not an hour out of Savannah when the truck was weaving and a tire exploded because of all the weight from the paint cans. The truck rolled over and there was paint all over the road. Ted's mom started screaming because she thought Jane was dead because of the accident. The red paint looked like blood and she was afraid her daughter was dead. After sometime, Jane emerged from the totaled-out truck covered in red paint with out a scratch on her body. That was a sigh of relief. At that point they did not care the truck was totaled-out.

When Ted was a kid, his dad painted many barns. He had a hired man that worked with him between 1-2 years. One day the hired man said that he had to quit because he was going to the army. At this time Ted was 11 years old. Ted's dad needed help, so his mother said to his father, "Take Ted with you". Ted was then helping his father paint barns. They painted the barn with these spray guns. One barn in particular was very high and there was a section of the high point that no one could reach. His dad said, "Ted you hold on to the ladder and I will slide it up so you can reach the high spot". Well, Ted's dad took this 36 foot wooden ladder and put it against his chest and slid it to the high area. Ted was hanging on for dear life shaking like a leaf on a tree. Ted's dad then hollered up, "Can you reach it now"? Holding on the ladder with one hand and the sprayer with the other, Ted finished painting the highest point of the barn. He was relieved when he got off the ladder. Even the farmer was impressed how Ted got the highest point of the barn painted. A traveler did anything to get the job done. Neither Ted nor his dad saw the entire danger of holding the ladder so high in the air. However, Ted had complete confidence in his 41 year old father.

Ted personally experienced prejudice and hatred because he was a traveler. As mentioned prior, some travelers had a bad reputation. Ted was painting roofs with black tar at this point in the March of 1964. The tar would preserve the asphalt shingles. Someone accused Ted of cheating him. They called him a Williamson which was a derogatory name. Ted was put in jail for three days. Someone told him to hire the ex-prosecuting attorney to win the case. Ted did not cheat the man and did what he said he was going to do. Ted did not go up in price and did the work properly. Even the FBI checked out the case and there was nothing done wrong. Judges had a reputation of throwing the book at travelers. The people who made false accusations against Ted knew he was innocent but did not give up. Ted's lawyer said, "Do you know they have false accusations against you? Let's sue them and you could own the farm". Ted said, "No, I just want to get out of this situation, as a traveler I don't want any trouble". Ted then pled guilty just to get out of these false accusations. Everything was dropped but Ted and his uncle Martin had to pay $26.00 each for court costs, and one year probation.

Chapter 4

The Fighter

Ted's grandfather and father taught Ted to box at the age of 15. He was taught how to do left hooks and right hooks. They taught him how to throw an upper cut, left jab, and a right cross.

When Ted hit him on the button, it was his chin. It was the punch that could knock someone out. Ted's dad taught him more than throwing punches; it was also about respect. Ted's dad said, "Never take advantage of anyone. I'd rather have you take a beating than take advantage of someone". One day Mickey Riley was drunk and said something that insulted Ted. Ted got upset and hit Mickey in the mouth. Ted's dad got upset with Ted because he hit Mickey. Ted's dad said, "That poor bugger did not want to fight you. You hit him for nothing". Again, Ted learned another lesson from his dad. John Gorman took it up with Ted for hitting Mickey Riley. John and Ted fought for about 10 minutes and things were settled.

In the summer of 1952 Ted lived in Spring Lake Michigan. Ted was 15 years old. One night, Ted's dad went bowling with some friends in Spring Lake. In those days the bowling alley had pin boys set up the pins after the bowling ball was tossed down the lane. The pin boy thought one of the bowlers was tossing the ball too quickly and he became upset. He did not know who it was so he took his anger out on his father. He harassed

his father and called him nasty names. One night, Ted was at the bowling alley and someone said to the pin boy that Ted was the son of the guy he harassed a couple days earlier. The pin boy was 17 years old, 170 pounds, 5' 11" and a golden glove boxer. Ted was only 5' 7" and 135 pounds. Needless to say, a fight started. Ted had a great left jab and the fists were flying. Ted backed him up a city block and knocked him down. The pin boy's brother said, "Don't let that so and so beat you." The pin boy said, "I'm blind in one eye and can't see out of the other, I have to quit". Ted pounded on him a little longer and the fight was over. All the friends that Ted went to the bowling alley with walked home. They were talking about the fight and how great Ted beat up the golden glove boxer. They made Ted feel like he was the champion of the world. It was a tremendous feeling for Ted and a great experience for all his friends.

In 1956 Ted lived in Steubenville Ohio. Ted worked out in the gym 2-3 days a week with some of the best boxers in the nation. He worked out with John Harper and Walter Ingrem. John Harper was a heavy weight champion and Walter Ingrem was featherweight champion at 135 pounds. Joe Peron was the trainer/manager. One day 5 fighters and the trainer had to go to Pittsburg Pennsylvania for a fight. Ted also wanted to go along. The manager's car broke down. Ted had a 1956 Buick that his dad bought for him. Joe agreed to let Ted drive the group to Pittsburg for the fight. Ted had a wonderful time in Pittsburg. There he met more professional fighters including Bob Baker, the Zivic brothers, and Billy Conn who almost beat Joe Lewis.

Ted worked out in the gym with the fighters in Steubenville Ohio. Walter Ingrem was one of the best fighters they had at that time in Steubenville. Walter was in the ring and the trainer, Joe Peron, asked Walter to go 1 round with Ted Daley.

He agreed to one round. Joe wrapped up Ted's hands and put on the gloves. Walter said, I'm only going one round with you Ted". You see, Walter figured he would knock Ted out in just a couple of seconds. Ted was tougher than Walter thought. Ted hit him with a couple of rights and lefts. He dodged him a few times. Walter hit Ted with a left hook but then made a huge mistake as he dropped his left hand a bit that gave Ted the opportunity to throw a right punch right to his button. Ted was about 155 pounds and Walter was 135 pounds. Ted lifted him right off the ground and he was flying through the air; it must have been 10 feet. One must understand that there were 25 men working out in the gym at that same time. When Walter hit the floor, you could hear a pin drop. Everyone was looking at what just happened. Walter was not on the floor very long; he jumped up with fire in his eyes. Now he wanted to kill Ted. Lucky for Ted the round was just about over. Walter came back and hit Ted about as hard as Ted has ever been hit in his life. He hit Ted with a right hook on the side of his face and almost knocked Ted down. The bell rang and the round was over. Walter was so fired up that he said, "Let's go another round". Then trainer Joe Peron said, "No, No! Ted is not in shape and you know that! Let him get in shape and he can fight you. He knows what he is doing. Then I will let you go 3 rounds with him". Ted got out of the ring and took off his gloves. Walter was upset that he would not go another round with him.

The manager said, "Do you know what you just did? You just decked Walter Ingrem! There is not a man in the State of Ohio that could deck Walter; I don't care how good they are. He works out with that heavy weight John Harper, and John Harper can't deck him. And if he can't no one can hit him". That was a plus for Ted Daley.

Ted worked out a couple more weeks in Steubenville Ohio. During that time, he got to know more of the fighters. Ted took some of the fighters to other places with his nice fancy Buick car. The travelers liked nice cars. GM said that the travelers were the best customers as a group.

One night in the gym, Joe Peron, the trainer, said that Ted could turn pro if he made welter weight. Ted went home and told his father that he wanted to be a professional fighter. His brother in law heard this news and went down to the gym to talk with Joe Peron. Martin asked Joe, "just how good is Ted"? Joe said, "Yes, he has all the moves. He hits hard and he knows how to throw a punch. We think he can make some money in the fighting game". Joe goes on to say, "We call him a natural fighter. With what he knows now I believe with more training he can be the welter weight champion of the world in a couple of years". Those words made Ted really feel good. Ted recalled when he was 11 years old, he had several fights and he won them all. Some of the fights he won were against amateur fighters.

Shortly after uncle Martin's talk with Joe Peron, Ted's dad had a long conversation with Ted. Ted's dad said, "Son, fighting is no life for a traveler. Look at all the Irish travelers who were fighters. Nothing came of it. Look at Jimmy Hutchenson who was a great fighter in the 20's, Obow Williams in the 30's, Bradley from Texas, John Daugherty from California; they never ended up pursuing it. You will end up getting your brains beat right out of your head". Ted said, "This man said I was good". His dad said, "I believe you, but this is no life for a traveler. I wish you would not do it". Ted said, "I could not go against my father. Ted then left Steubenville Ohio in a couple of weeks and gave up his boxing career. After that time, even though Ted did not get paid for his boxing abilities, he still engaged in some street fights.

Chapter 5
The Fighter Continues

I n 1964 Ted lived in Chicago. He did many different jobs to make a living, as did many travelers. A couple of the many jobs that Ted did was putting slate on house roofs and seal coated driveways. Ted had a cousin by the name of Lawrence on his mother's side of the family. It was funny that Ted's own sister,  Jane, kicked the hell out of Lawrence when he was 12 years old. Lawrence grew up to be a great fighter. In fact, Lawrence beat the toughest man in Terran County Texas in 1953. One must understand the grit of Lawrence to really appreciate the huge feat that Ted accomplished when he fought Lawrence.

Ted was 15 years old in 1953. Lawrence was 22 or 23 years old at that time. Many Irish travelers would go drinking at the bar after a long day of work. One day there were a group of 10-12 Irish travelers who went to the Parish Inn in Fort Worth Texas. One of the guys in the bar was Glenn Greyson. Glenn was the toughest man in Terran County Texas. Glenn was 6' tall and 240 pounds. Glenn said, "I can beat anyone in the house for $100.00". Glenn went to every person in the bar and said, "I can beat you, and you and you". John Daley, an Irish traveler said, "I thought all you sons of bitches left". Before John got those words out of his mouth Lawrence said, "I'll fight you. I don't have $100.00 on me, but I will fight you for nothing". Glenn Greyson said to another guy, "Tell him who I am, tell him who I am! Don't you know that I'm the great Glenn Greyson"? Lawrence then said, "I don't give a shit who you are. I can beat you in two minutes". At that time Lawrence was 6' and 185 pounds; but in good shape. Glenn said, "Oh ya, you think you can beat me"? As Glenn was leaving the bar, Glenn grabbed Lawrence's shoulder then hit him in his button. Lawrence went flying back through the air maybe 10 feet. As he was laying on the ground, he said, "Don't kick me. I'll fight you. Let me get back up". Glenn then said, "I should have kicked your stupid head off. Glenn Greyson can beat a dozen of wimps of the likes of you". Glenn made the mistake of letting Lawrence get up off the floor. Now the fight really began. They fought for 15-20 minutes. Glenn never hit Lawrence again. Lawrence kept going for his belly. Lawrence would give him a right had to his guts then come back with a left jab. Glenn was all busted up. Glen then said, "Let old Glenn rest a little bit. Boy you are good. You can really fight". Lawrence said, "I don't need any rest. You are beat. You have to understand there was a big crowd in this bar. Some in the crowd were saying, "Make him say he is beat"! Glenn said, I will fight you some more. Just let me get my wind back". Lawrence said, "I don't need me wind back". Then Lawrence hit him again with an upper cut. Lawrence knocked him in a flower planter. By then, Glenn was finished.

Within the huge crowd that was there, many were making side bets on the fight. There were gangsters in the place that called themselves the Texas Mafia. One of the gangsters hit Lawrence in the head with a bottle. Ted even got hit in the head and was staggering around. Ned tried to help Ted. Happy Jack had a razor-sharp knife with a blade 8-10 inches long. Happy Jack cut the button off of Lawrence's suit and put it in his side. Ted thought he was dying because he was breathing so heavy. Now there were three fights going on all at the same time. The entire bar was in chaos. Someone called the ambulance. Before the ambulance arrived, Danny McCombe ran up to Lawrence 2-3 times and screamed at Lawrence and said, "You cost me $100.00". You see, Danny bet on Glenn Greyson, but Lawrence won the fight. The ambulance arrived and Lawrence was brought to the hospital because of the knife wound. Lawrence got sewed up.

The above fight shows the heart, strength and toughness of Lawrence. He knew how to fight.

In those days, many Irish Travelers did not put money in the bank. In the summer of 1964, there was a rumor going on that Lawrence stole uncle Jim's money. One must also understand that Ted loved Lawrence and saw him as a big brother. Because of that relationship, Ted was the only relative who could set the rumor straight if Lawrence really took the money from uncle Jim.

Many travelers liked to gather at the Congress Inn in Chicago to have a few beers. One night, Ted, Lawrence and Alex were in the bar at the Congress Inn. Ted was actually scared of Lawrence. While in the bar, Ted asked Lawrence, "Lawrence, did you take uncle Jim's money". Lawrence said, "would you ask me that if it was Finney's money (Finney was his mother's maiden name) instead of Daley's money"? Ted said, "Yes I would". Lawrence then said, "Well, I ain't going to tell you"! Ted said, "Lawrence, you are either going to tell me or you are going to have to fight me". After he said that Ted was really scared and had a lump in his throat. Even if I got beat, I would now have to fight him. Well, the fight started.

Going out of the bar Ted caught him under his right hand with his left hand. I kept him off balance. Ted knew that if he hit him with his left hook, Ted would be somewhere in Disneyland. They both went out the door and Lawrence stepped off the curb. Lawrence was about 2-3 inches taller than Ted. Now that he stepped off the curb, they were the same height. Lawrence said, "I need to take a leak". Lawrence took a leak and turned to Ted and said, "Ted, I don't want to fight you". At this point Ted went too far, and was too nerved up. Ted threw his right hand directly into his button. Lawrence went out like a light. Lawrence fell at Ted's feet, but Ted did not know he was out. Ted thought he was playing possum. Ted said, "Get up, get up! Are you a coward? Get up and fight like a man. Don't do that to me". Lawrence was out for a good 10-15 seconds.

When Lawrence finally got up, he fought life a wild caged animal. He hit my head and put lumps on it. Ted was able to get away from him. Ted was holding his own as they continued to fight. Ted was 175 pounds and Lawrence was 230 pounds. The fighting went back and forth. Lawrence however, was out of shape. Ted backed him up to a stairway. There was a 15 foot drop from the top of the banister. Ted thought maybe he could throw him over the banister and the fight would be over. When the fight started Ted thought to himself, "kill or be killed". Either Lawrence was going to beat him to death, or Ted would knock him to his death. Just as Ted backed him up against the banister, Lawrence had an opening and turned him around and now Ted was backed up against the banister. Lawrence now had Ted half way over the banister. Ted grabbed him and held on for dear life. While holding on to either the banister or Lawrence, the fight continued. The fighting continued to go back and forth. Ted was afraid of falling 15 feet. As Ted was holding on to Lawrence, he bit Ted's middle finger. Ted had his right arm around his back and Lawrence had his left arm around Ted's back. Ted wanted to do some damage, but he bit his fingers. Ted pulled and pulled and finally got his finger loose. Then Lawrence got him down on the concrete. At this time, they were fighting for about 6-7 minutes, but it seemed a lot longer. Lawrence got on top of him and put his arm on his back. Lawrence then said, "Take an oath on your mother that you will quit fighting me if I let you up". Ted said, "No"! Lawrence then pounced on him again. He continued to have his arm against his back. Lawrence then pounded Ted's head against the concrete surface. Ted then said, "All right, I will take an oath on my mother". (Lawrence had respect for Ted's mother. Lawrence's mom and Ted's mom were sisters.) Then Lawrence said, "Get up". Ted said, "I ain't going to fight you until the morning". Lawrence walked away and was out of gas. He turned his back to Ted. Ted still had a little gas left in him and had a chance to hit him, but he just couldn't do it. Ted thought too much of him to hit him when he was turned away. Ted then walked away. Ted went home and taped up his fingers where Lawrence bit him. His wife Susan said, "What have you been doing"? Ted said, "I have been fighting Lawrence. I worked him up and I want to get over there the first thing in the morning". Ted then washed all the blood off himself and tried to heal from the fight that day.

Jim Daley used to say, "If you have trouble with someone in the night, make sure you get there the first thing in the morning". Well, dawn broke about 6:00 the next morning and Ted was at Lawrence's door. Ted banged on the door as hard as he can. Lawrence opened the door and said, "Oh, you crazy bastard. You damn near broke my jaw". Then he went on to say, "I did not take your uncle's money. Come on, I should have told you that I did not take your uncle's money". From that time on it was not like little brother talking to big brother. It was like two adult men talking things over. He swore to me that he did not take uncle Jim's money. I took him on his word. To this day there is still doubt if he took the money.

In 1973 Ted and couple of his cousins were playing cards with some of the southern travelers. Things got heated at one point and a fight broke out. There were seven southern travelers versus Ted and his cousin. Two of the southern travelers locked themselves in the bathroom to get away from this fight. There was no contest for Ted and his cousin as the 5 southern travelers got beat badly.

In 1976 Ted was in Florida. He was playing a pick-up game of basketball with Davey Moore and Woody Gorman. Ted was known as the bomb because he would blow up. Woody and Ted had some kind of disagreement and started to argue. Ted asked Woody if he could fight. Just then, Davey stepped in between Ted and Woody and looked Ted right into the eyes and said "I can fight". Davey took Woody's side. For some reason, Ted plugged Davey right between the eyes, and knocked him flat on his back. As he lay on the ground, he could hardly move. Davey was a runner and in good shape and weighed 175 pounds. Ted was 190 pounds. Earlier Davey said he could fight, but as he lay on the ground he did not want to fight anymore. Later, Ted went to the coffee shop but Davey did not show up to have a cup of coffee. A couple days later Ted saw Davey at a car wash. Davey said, "I'm ashamed of you, that with your reputation and ability that you would hit me". Ted said, "I would not have hit you if you would not have put yourself into a position to be hit". Ted then put his 2 thumbs in his back pocket where he could pull them out fast to defend himself if he had to defend himself. Ted then said, "Well, we all have to do what we gotta do". At this time Davey was with another big fella with a huge ring on his finger. The big guy walked up closer to Ted and threatened him. When he got closer, he changed his mind and walked away. He knew there would be trouble.

About 2 weeks later Ted was at a big shopping center in Tampa Bay Florida. There was a big drug store that Ted was entering located in that shopping center. Just before going into that drug store, Ted noticed a truck with some painting on the door. Ted did not notice who was driving or riding in that truck. Ted would have recognized them if they were other travelers, because travelers recognized one another. The bible passage that came to Ted's mind was from the gospel of John 10:14; I am the Good Shepherd. I know my sheep and my sheep know me. Ted knows the travelers and the travelers know Ted, even if they do not know their names. Ted then walked in the drug store. Shortly thereafter, those riding in that painted truck walked in; Harry Cooper and his 2 sons. Harry said, "Hay, how are you"? Ted did not respond because he did not know him. Harry then proceeds to mouth off to Ted and says, "I thought you were one of those sons of bitches that would not say hello to anybody. Ted then said, "I am not. I'm sorry. I did not know who you were. I sure would have said hello to you if I knew you". Harry said, "You can take it anyway you want". At this point Ted felt threatened. Ted then took off his watch and put it in his pocket.

Ted was by himself. The drug store had a mini restaurant and sitting at the booth in the restaurant were: John Birch, Buddy Goreman, and Tom Hamilton. These guys observed the whole incident. Ted then proceeded to engage Harry. Ted looked at him and said, "Well Harry, there is only one way to take it. We need to take it outside". They were about one half way outside and Harry got scared. Harry said, "Well Ted, we are travelers, let's forget about it". Once we got that far outside Ted could not forget about it. The bomb could not hold back any longer. The bomb exploded inside of Ted. Ted looked at him and threw his watch on the ground. His fuse went off and Ted plugged him. He co-cocked him so hard he hit the wall. They went out of the store as Ted continued to give him his famous left jab. Then he heard some screaming from the distance getting closer. It was Harry's son Harry Lee. Harry Lee was coming through the crowd with fire in his eyes. At the time Ted was 39 years old and Harry Lee was 22 years old. Harry Lee was 6'3" and 240 pounds. He was a strong young man built like Tarzan.

Now Ted and Harry Lee got into the fight. They fought and fought. Ted hardly remembers that incident because he was wound up so tight. Ted also believes the Holy Spirit was with him. So many people later told Ted that he must have hit him over 50 times. Harry Lee stepped off the curb from the drug store. There must have been a 1 ½ foot drop off into the parking lot. Ted grabbed him and then kneed him a couple of times. Ted then hit him a few more times and he fell flat on his back. His head hit the concrete like a basketball. Ted looked at him and saw he was knocked out. Now Harry Lee's brother Danny came running through the crowd and hit Ted. The crowd was gathering and things were getting out of hand. Ted now was defending himself against Danny. Fists were flying everywhere and the crowd was going nuts. Out of the crowd came another guy directly to Ted. The guy said he was an off-duty police officer. The off-duty officer asked Ted, "Do you want to get out of this"? Ted said, "Yes"! In the meantime, the father of the sons asked Ted, "Did you have enough"? Ted said, "No, Harry, I'll see you again". Harry got so upset that he hit Ted with everything he could. That punch did not even phase Ted. Ted turned his head to Harry and again said, "I'll see you again".

In the meantime, someone called the cops. Harry and his two sons were scared. Harry and Danny took off out of the parking lot. Harry Lee was carted off to the hospital because he was so badly beat up. The off-duty police officer told Ted, "You go through there". Ted ran through between two buildings to an area behind the drug store. No one got arrested that day. Through this fight everyone got to know Ted Daley. Again, Ted was out numbered. He fought a father and two sons on the same day. Ted to this day continues to believe that God was with him to win the fight that day.

Two weeks later Ted pulled in the seal coat plant in Tampa Bay Florida. Ted was driving a one-ton truck. Sitting in the truck with Ted was his cousin Pete. Ironically, at that exact same time, Harry, Harry Lee, and Danny were at the seal coat plant. Harry was on the back of the truck and his boys were aside of the truck. Also, inside Harry's truck was Harry's son in law, and a dog named Satan. Cousin Pete, with a cast on his foot, went to the seal coat plant office, leaving Ted alone in the truck. Pete thought Ted could beat 10 men like Harry in one day. Ted did not know what to do. Harry's truck was about 30 feet away from Ted's truck. Harry then said, "What do you want to do Daley? Do you want to fight, shake hands or forget about it"? Ted then said, "I just assume to shake hands and forget all about it, because I did not want to fight in the first place." Ted knew if he could beat the 3 men again, he would not be able to get past Satan, the Doberman pinscher. Harry now walked closer to Ted's truck. Harry was a little apprehensive because he did not know what Ted had in his truck. Maybe Ted had a gun or some other weapon. Harry then stops and turns to Harry Lee and said, "What do you want to do". Harry Lee was pretty sore and looked marbly purple. Harry Lee said, "I want to shake hands and forget about it". Ted then agreed and said, "Let's forget all about it". Ted was then relieved and blessed himself. Ted then got more seal coat product, picked up John and drove off to the next job.

There were times when Ted was called in to make sure a fight was fair. Billy Core, a Catholic Irish traveler, married a protestant girl. They were having marriage problems and Ted felt sorry for Billy. The girl's uncle Charlie was not happy with the situation. A number of travelers got together at the pool hall in Hollywood. Ted got in the car with Billy. Somehow, they knew there would be a fight. Billy wanted Ted to be there to make sure the fight was fair on both sides. Charlie and Billy started arguing and a fight started. Billy wanted to get his wife back. A number of travelers were on the hill watching the fight. At the end of the fight Billy got the best of Charlie. Ted raised Billy's hand in the sign of victory, and the travelers cheered. Charlie was a cousin of Ted and Charlie did not speak to Ted for years. Some years later they got back together.

There were other times that Ted did not want any fights to start. In fact, he wanted to stop them. In the fall of 1963 Ted was seal coating driveways in California. Ted and Charlie Holiday were in one truck, and George and Pete Daley were in another truck. All were at the seal coat plant picking up sealer. On that particular day there were 60-70 men at the plant at the same time. A fight broke out between the Scottish travelers; Sonny McMillen and Tommy James. There was a split between the huge crowd that gathered in that place. One half was on the side of Sonny and the other half was on the side of Tommy. One guy picked up a hammer, another a pipe and other things just laying on the ground. Some people started to back away because the situation was getting tense. Ted saw a chance to stop the fight. Ted knew most of the people there knew his father, and he too wanted to be noticed. Ted then jumped up on his truck and started singing' "Hay, look me over lend me an ear. Fresh out of clover and mortgage up to here". After that song, Ted said, "Look out world, here I come". Charlie, the guy riding with Ted was scared because he thought the crowd would come after them. At that time a big man putting sealer on the truck said, "Hay, that's it". Then he started clapping. Then Flip, the guy selling sealer, started clapping. Then Richie, a Scottish traveler, said, "Ya, that's it". The two guys fighting stopped to listen to the song Ted was singing. Someone said, "Let's forget about things. If they have a disagreement, the heck with it". Someone else hollered at Ted and said, "Thanks for singing that song". Everyone laughed and got into their trucks and went to work. The fight was finished and things ended peacefully. Ted was happy how things ended that day. The song broke up the whole fight. Ted then wrote, "The power of a Song".

Throughout Ted's life he encountered many people in fights of different sorts. Ted did not loose one of his fights. The boxing community recognized his accomplishments by inducting Ted Daley in the Bare Knuckle Hall of Fame on July 8, 2017 in Belfast New York. There was a ceremony for the induction. People in charge of the ceremony found out that Ted could sing. The organizers of the ceremony asked Ted to sing a couple of songs. Ted was also a singer in his own right.

Chapter 6

The Singer

When Ted was 10 years old one of his cousins from England, George Finney, came to visit his grandparents in Chicago. Ted's family decided to take a trip to Chicago to visit the Finney family. This was the first time Ted met George. In the course of the visit George started singing.

Ted's dad heard him sing and Ted wanted to learn how to sing. George was an awesome singer. Ted's dad encouraged Ted also to start singing. Ted, for many years, was afraid to stand up in crowds and perform. However, after some years after growing up, when Ted and some friends got together at a local pub, they would sing some songs. Singing songs in a pub was very common in those days. Ted got better and better at singing and he was able to build up his confidence.

In 1965 Ted was living in a motel apartment in Santa Clara California with other travelers. Ted's wife and 2 children were also living in the motel apartment. A number of travelers lived together and picked up jobs while living in the area. Ted seal coated driveways and other black topped surfaces. On St. Patrick's Day many Irish travelers got together at the motel lounge. Ted got up and started singing many Irish songs on St. Patrick's Day. The owner and manager of the motel was Joe Ferriero. Joe heard Ted sing many songs and was really impressed. Joe went up to Ted and said, "Say, you can really sing". Joe then asked Ted, "Would you like to go to Reno and make a demo?" Ted said, "Sure!" Joe was well connected with people in show business and the music industry. Joe then took Ted to Reno to Reprize Records to make a demo. Ted made the demo and it worked out very well. Joe Ferriero then took Ted all around San Francisco California, to different night clubs and lounges, where he performed. He even performed at a bowling alley where that eccentric owner was big in the mafia. All the night clubs and lounges that Joe took Ted to were Italian. The bowling alley had a huge lounge and the place was packed. Ted sang for this huge crowd and one of the microphones went dead. Ted naturally reached for the other mic and finished the song. As Ted was done and going to his table Joe came up to Ted and said "They shut the one microphone off on purpose to see how you would react. You passed the test. You did what you were supposed to do". Ted did not perform professionally like this before, but now Ted was moving up in the music world. The more Ted was singing in these clubs and lounges, the more he thought the industry was run by the mafia. Joe told Ted that he needed an Italian name. Joe said that he was going to give him the name Danny Ferriero. Ted was also assured that if he did well, Ted would have all the women he wanted. Ted was getting more and more nervous the deeper he got into his singing career. Ted was actually scared.

After the weather got better up north in Seattle Washington, Ted and his family moved back to Seattle. There, Ted and his family lived in another motel and worked on seal coating driveways in that area. That was the life of a traveler. Ted's mother and aunt lived in Santa Clara California. On Mother's Day, Ted decided to fly down to Santa Clara to see his mother and talk to Joe Ferriero.

Back in California Joe Ferriero built a big fancy night club called The Golden Door in a very ritzy neighborhood in Santa Clara. The plan was to have fashion shows at The Golden Door during the day and Ted would sing at night. On Mother's Day, Ted did visit his mother and also checked out the new night club; The Golden Door. Joe showed Ted around the brand new night club; it was grand opening weekend. Joe then met with a group of men in the back room of this fancy building. He made Ted believe it was big time mafia. Ted was getting even more scared. Joe then led Ted to this back room. There were men in there with big heads of hair, just like in the movies. Ted took a seat at the table with these guys and his stomach was turning. He did not sense things were going well. Joe was also on the side sitting on a chair. One of the guys around the table leaned forward and said, "I'm going to tell you something, I'd advise you that you do everything this guy tells you to do. (He was pointing to Joe) This guy is going to put a lot of money into you, so you better do as he says." He also said to Ted, "You need to send your wife and kids back to Texas. It would be better if you were a single man". Now Ted was really getting scared not only for himself but for his entire family. Ted's mind was racing. He was wondering what he got himself into. First Joe wanted to change his name. Ted did not want his name changed. He wanted to be known as Ted Daley, an Irish traveler. Now these guys are making threatening demands of him. Well, Ted left The

Golden Door, because he was so scared. From the time Ted arrived in Santa Clara to the time he left the place was only about 1 ½ hours. Ted did not even eat a meal at the place. Ted's mother and aunt took him back to the airport where he flew back to Seattle Washington to be with his wife and kids.

Many of the travelers stuck together, regardless if they were Catholic or protestant. Ted seemed to know them all throughout the United States. A Scotch traveler, George Johnson Sr. died. He lived near Las Angeles California. Ted was called to attend the funeral because of his friendship with George. The family even asked Ted to be a pall bearer. Ted accepted, and wore a green coat representing all of George's Irish traveler friends. The ceremony took place at the beautiful chapel at Forest Lawn Cemetery. There was a visitation the night before the funeral. During the wake service Ted sang the song; Amazing Grace. After he finished singing the song, Ted received a standing ovation from those gathered that evening in the chapel. The next morning, Esther, a friend of Ted's, said, "Ted, keep up your singing. Do you know you touched everyone in the chapel last night? The Holy Spirit is in your voice. Don't stop singing".

The funeral that next day at Forest Lawn cemetery was like that out of the movies. Nothing was too good for George Johnson Sr. There were two white horses pulling a horse drawn carriage. The driver of the horses wore a black top hat. They were going up a hill and you could see the entire area. The day was picture perfect at 70 degrees and not a breath of wind blowing. There were between 150 – 175 people in attendance. Ted was standing between George's wife and his son. After the minister was done saying his prayers, Ted could not hold back and started singing the Prayer of St. Francis. The Prayer of St. Francis goes as follows: Make me a channel of your peace. Where there is hatred, let me bring your love. Where there is injury, your pardon, Lord. And where there's doubt, true faith in you. Make me a channel of your peace. Where there's despair in life, let me bring hope. Where there is darkness, only light. And when there's sadness, ever joy. O Master, grant that I may never seek so much to be consoled, as to console, to be understood as to understand, to be loved, as to love with all my soul. Make me a channel of your peace. It is in pardoning, that we are pardoned, in giving of ourselves that we receive, and in dying that we are born to eternal life. After the song there was complete silence as if everyone was soaking in the Holy Spirit. Many people came up to Ted after the service and shook his hand and thanked him for adding so much to the ceremony.

Ted also sang for family gatherings. One of Ted's granddaughters attended college at Colorado University. At the university she fell in love with a man from England whose father was a professor in Scotland. Because of the family connection, the wedding took place in the chapel at Glasgow University in Scotland. The president told Ted that the university was the second oldest university in the world. As part of the wedding ceremony Ted sang The Prayer of St. Francis. The Dean of the university was in attendance at the wedding. He was so impressed with Ted's singing ability that he came up to Ted after the wedding ceremony and gave him a beautiful coin. It was the size of a half dollar. That coin was a true memento for the privilege to sing in such of a prestigious university on such a special occasion of a granddaughter's wedding.

Ted was involved in local community events where he was able to utilize his talents. Ted was seal coating driveways and parking lots in Northern Wisconsin. He was known as the singing seal coater because he would sing on the local radio station when he advertised for his business. Many restaurants where he and his wife frequented knew who he was and they would ask him to sing a song right there in the establishment. Some community leaders recognized Ted's singing from the radio and mentioned to him how they heard his singing. The same community leaders asked Ted if he could act as well as sing. The woman behind the bar spoke up and said, "Ted has been acting all his life". The community leaders then asked Ted if he would be involved in the community play. Ted agreed to participate in the play and became a hit with his singing and acting.

Ted also has recorded singing a number of familiar songs. One is able to access some of his musical style on youtube under Ted Daley. Among some of his songs are Mona Lisa and Danny Boy.

Ted also sang at boxing events. Bobby Gunn was a professional fighter. Ted got to know Bobby and became good friends. Bobby then asked Ted to sing the National Anthem at many of his boxing matches. Ted sang for10-12 of Bobby Gunn's fights. One of the most famous fights Ted sang for was when Bobby Gunn fought Roy Jones. The fight took place in Wilmington Delaware on February 17 2017. There were over 5000 people in the arena for the fight. The fight also was nationally televised as well as in 40 different countries. Ted sang the national anthem with gusto. Later Bobby Gunn received calls as far as Australia, England and Ireland wondering who sang the national anthem. Ted even sang personally for the heavy weight champion of the world Tyson Fury. Bobby Gunn was instrumental in helping Ted enter the Bare Knuckle Hall of Fame. Ted had a knack of connecting with the popular and famous people, which we will introduce next.

Chapter 7

Ted Meets Famous People

Jack Dempsey

The life of a traveler was not easy. Travelers' worked hard at a number of jobs to provide for their families. Throughout Ted's life he did a variety of jobs including; seal coating driveways and parking lots, installing lightening rods on barns and houses, applying linseed oil on wooden fences and painting barns. Ted's dad had a gift in selling things. Ted inherited that gift from his dad. Ted had no problem going to someone's home, ring the door bell and initiating a conversation. He enjoyed meeting many different people. Of course, he would run across some challenging ones. If there was a popular or famous person in the area, he liked to approach them for a job. He thought it was a treat and privilege to land a job with them. There were other times and circumstances where Ted would either run into or seek out interesting people in which he would interact with a popular person.

Tyson fury, the heavyweight champion of the world

One of those times was the day Ted was flying from Santa Clara California back to Seattle Washington. As Ted was in the airport, he ran into Jack Werner from Werner Brothers Studios. Ted said, "Mr. Werner, I saw you a couple of nights ago on the Andy Williams Show". Ted then went on to tell Jack Werner how he was singing and he wanted to tell him about the travelers. Ted asked for an address, and Mr. Werner told Ted to write to Bill Schafer, his manager. In turn, Bill would make sure he got the letter. Ted did write to him about the life of a traveler.

In the summer of 1971 Ted was working in Michigan. When Ted arrived in Berrien Springs Michigan, he met Mohammad Ali. Mohammad Ali, as you recall, was the Heavy Weight Champion Boxer of the World. Ted worked for Mohammad Ali by seal coating his driveway.

In the fall of 1971 Ted was living in Fort Worth Texas. Ray Price was a big name in country music at that time. Ted saw and visited with Ray. Ted sold and installed lightening rods on the home of Ray Price in Mt. Pleasant Texas. Ted thought if he could work for Ray Price, he could work for anyone.

In 1976 Ted met George Foreman on his ranch in East Texas. George also was a Heavy Weight Champion boxer of the World. George had a training facility in Marshall Texas. Ted even went to the gym where George worked out. Ted not only sold and installed lightening rods on George's house, but also installed rods on the house of George's mother. Many years later, around 1981, Ted ran into George. At that time, he was no longer fighting professionally. However, Ted ran into him watching a fight in that area. Ted, again, reminisced with him about the job of installing lightening rods many years prior.

In 1981 Ted was working in the Oklahoma City Oklahoma area. Dale Robertson was a famous movie star that lived in Yukon Oklahoma. Ted sold and installed lightening rods on the home of Dale Robertson.

Also, in 1981, Ted met Tony Dorsett. Tony Dorsett was the famous running back for the Dallas Cowboys in the late 1970's. Ted applied linseed oil to the wood fence that surrounded his property.

In the fall of 1984 Ted was living in the New Yorker Trailer Park in New Jersey. Ted found out where Jacqueline Kennedy Onassis lived. Jacqueline had a summer cottage near Peapack New Jersey. Jacqueline boarded her jumping horse on that property with Murry McDonald. Ted worked for a farmer, John Smith, who had property that boarders the private road of the Kennedy property. John Smith gave permission to Ted to use that road to speak to Mrs. Kennedy. Ted went there a dozen different times and could not catch her home. One day, however, Jacqueline was jogging and Ted then personally met her. Ted said, "Mrs. Kennedy, my name is Ted Daley. I sell and install lightening rods. I would like to do them for your house". Jacqueline then said, "Oh, don't I have them up already"? Ted then said, "I don't believe so". She then said, "Oh sure, put them on". Ted was so happy and excited that he got the job. He wasted no time and drove there within a few minutes with his materials and supplies. Ted drove up in the yard and the caretaker came running to his car and said, "What are you doing here"? Ted explained to the care taker of the property that Mrs. Kennedy gave permission to have the lightening rods installed. After a few minutes Jacqueline came out of the house and said to her caretaker, "What a nice boy. Let him put rods on the small guard house as well". Ted sent her the bill for the job. It was $850.00 for the house and $350.00 for the guard house. The check was to be sent to the trailer park where he lived. In the meantime, Ted went back to Texas. Ted's daughter was still living at the New Yorker Trailer Park. The day Ted's daughter received the check from Mrs. Kennedy, she called her dad and told him about the exciting news of receiving the check. The check was then sent down to the place where Ted was living in Texas. Ted received the check signed by Jacqueline Kennedy Onassis on the anniversary date of the death of John F. Kennedy. Ted thought this might be some mystical sign. Ted immediately drove down to the church, St. George, which he attended. He approached the pastor, Fr. Ronny Mathias, of St. George Church. Ted said, "Father, I have something I want to give to you". Fr. Mathias said, "Ted, you flabbergast me. This check is from Jacqueline Kennedy Onassis". Ted said, "Father, I would rather have you run the check through the church books and not my personal bank. I don't want any bad vibes coming from Texas, after all, what happened to her husband in Dallas. Please, do what you want with the money". Ted was happy it was going to a good cause.

That same summer Ted worked and lived in New York, he met James Cagney. James Cagney was the famous movie star, dancer, and singer. Ted drove to Stanfordville New York where he received better directions to the farm in Bagnall New York, where James Cagney lived. Don Zimmerman was Cagney's manager. Ted approached Mr. Zimmerman and asked to see Mr. Cagney. Don then introduced Ted to James Cagney and he said, "This guy is as Irish as Patty's Pig. He wants to put lightening rods on your house". Mr. Cagney then said, "Well, you might just as well let him". Ted enjoyed the conversation and shook hands with him. Ted, again, felt honored to do the work for James Cagney. All the people that Ted worked for enriched Ted's life in a very positive way.

In the summer of 1994 Ted was working in Montana. Ted ran into the movie actress Andie McDowell. She lived on a beautiful ranch near French Lake Montana. Ted sold and installed copper lightening protection on a big barn on the ranch. Ted accidentally left the gate open by the barn and the horses got out of the pen. There was a guy working on the ranch that tried to get the horses back in the gate, but failed. Ted stopped his work and rounded up the horses and got them in their stalls without any problems. The employee at the ranch could not believe how good Ted handled those horses.

Ted also enjoyed the hospitality of many towns and cities throughout the United States. One of those towns was Memphis Tennessee. From 1990-1998 Ted would visit John Chillie Riley on St. Patrick's Day who lived in Memphis. John set it up where Ted was the Grand Marshall of the St. Patrick's Day parade in Memphis for those 8 years. Ted sang for the mayor of Memphis. The mayor gave Ted a symbolic key to the city and made him an honorary citizen of Shelby County Tennessee.

Ted truly believes he had a blessed life. The day the Holy Spirit came into his heart was one of the greatest days of his life. Many people told Ted that God had a plan for his life. Ted was not sure of the plan as he lived his life, however, as Ted looks back at 85 years, he sees how God was with him and he was able to appreciate that plan. His life was filled with experiences that he never dreamt possible. Ted hopes his legacy will continue long after he is gone from this wonderful place. As Ted, the Irish traveler, travels on, he hopes more people take advantage of the opportunities that are given to them and show respect to one another to make this world a better place. Wherever Ted experienced life as a traveler, he left that place a better place. Not only the physical place, but also the place in our hearts. Ted wishes to thank you for spending this time on his journey as an Irish traveler. He wants to leave you with the Irish Blessing as you continue your travels to the place we call heaven. May the road rise up to meet you. May the wind be always at your back. May the Sun shine warmly upon your face; The rains fall softly upon your fields. And, until we meet again, May God hold you in the palm of His hand.